How Grassroots Candidates Get Elected in Canada

Vanida Plamondon

HOW GRASSROOTS CANDIDATES GET ELECTED IN CANADA

First edition. December 2, 2024.

ISBN: 979-8230971610

Written by Vanida Plamondon.

Introduction

Grassroots candidates are the heartbeat of democracy. They remind us that politics doesn't have to be a game for the wealthy or well-connected. These are people who step into the political arena with little more than conviction and a willingness to roll up their sleeves. They don't lean on big corporations, wealthy donors, or political machines. Instead, they rely on their communities, real connections, and the belief that everyday people deserve a say in shaping their own futures. When a grassroots candidate runs for office, they're not just aiming to win a seat; they're challenging the idea that power belongs to those with the deepest pockets.

What makes grassroots candidates stand out is their refusal to be tied down by outside influences. They don't take money from corporations, foreign entities, or religious organizations that often expect favours in return. This freedom lets them focus on the needs of their constituents without juggling the interests of donors or political insiders. Their campaigns aren't built in boardrooms or fundraisers with a $500-per-plate price tag. They're built on doorsteps, in community centres, and during conversations at the local coffee shop. These candidates depend on small donations, volunteers, and the kind of grassroots momentum that comes when people feel genuinely heard and represented.

Historically, Canada has seen moments where grassroots efforts broke through and redefined what's possible in politics. These aren't the stories of candidates parachuted into constituencies by party brass. Instead, they're stories of people who grew from their communities and reflected their neighbours' values and priorities. Sometimes these candidates upset established political norms by proving that a message of authenticity and community-focused leadership resonates more than slick ads or party endorsements. It's a testament to how people-powered campaigns can challenge even the most entrenched systems.

There's something refreshing about watching a grassroots campaign take shape. It's scrappy and unpredictable but also deeply personal. These candidates don't often have the luxury of glossy marketing or extensive media coverage. They have conversations. They listen. They make themselves accessible in ways that career politicians often don't. This approach might lack polish, but it has heart. It reminds voters that democracy works best when it's close to the ground. The barriers to entry for grassroots candidates are steep, but their approach to politics is a crucial counterbalance to a system that can sometimes feel like it prioritizes dollars over people.

The essence of grassroots politics is the idea that change starts from the bottom up. It's not about waiting for someone in power to decide what's best for you. It's about stepping up and saying, "This is what our community needs, and I'm willing to fight for it." For me, that's the kind of leadership worth getting excited about.

Grassroots Candidates Still Win Elections

Grassroots candidates winning elections isn't some pie-in-the-sky idea. It's happening today. These candidates prove that you don't need big money or an established party machine to connect with voters. What they do need is strategy, and they've got that in spades. They know how to engage with their communities in ways that feel real. They know how to bring people together around shared goals. They know how to use media tools that anyone with a phone or computer can access. They're also smart about reading the political landscape and figuring out where the cracks are in the usual system. It's not magic. It's a mix of hard work, adaptability, and understanding people.

Community engagement is at the heart of what makes grassroots campaigns tick. It's not just about shaking hands and making speeches. It's about being present where people are, whether that's at a town hall, a farmers' market, or someone's front porch. Grassroots candidates don't wait for voters to come to them. They go out and meet voters where they live and work. It's exhausting and time-consuming, but it works. When people feel seen and heard, they're more likely to listen to what you have to say. They're also more likely to tell their neighbours, "Hey, you should check out this person. They actually get it."

Building coalitions is another powerful tool for grassroots candidates. They don't have the luxury of endless resources, so they rely on strength in numbers. This means working with community groups, unions, advocacy organizations, and even other political outsiders. It's about finding common ground and pooling resources to get things done. Historically, coalitions have been game-changers in Canadian politics. Whether it was the labour movement in the early 20th century or Indigenous communities rallying for representation, these alliances have shown that there's power in unity. Grassroots candidates tap into that same energy today, showing that when people come together around shared values, they can overcome even the toughest odds.

Alternative media has been a game-changer. In the past, if a candidate couldn't get the backing of major newspapers or TV networks, their voice could easily be drowned out. That's not the case anymore. Social media, blogs, podcasts, and even local independent news outlets have levelled the playing field. Grassroots candidates use these platforms to speak directly to voters, bypassing the filters of traditional media. It's not always polished, but it's authentic. People respond to that. They like hearing from a candidate without feeling like every word has been focus-grouped. This direct connection helps build trust and gives grassroots campaigns the visibility they need without the massive price tag of traditional advertising.

Staying adaptable in the face of political change is another hallmark of successful grassroots candidates. Canadian politics isn't static. Demographics shift, issues evolve, and the way people engage with politics changes. Grassroots candidates are often better at rolling with these changes than their more entrenched counterparts. They're closer to the ground, so they can sense when priorities are shifting and adjust their messaging and approach accordingly. Whether it's responding to a housing crisis, addressing climate concerns, or fighting for more equitable healthcare, they know how to align their campaigns with what matters most to voters right now. This kind of responsiveness is a big part of why they resonate with people in ways that more traditional campaigns sometimes don't.

It's inspiring to see grassroots candidates making it work. They're showing us that there's still room for authentic, people-driven politics in a system that often feels too focused on money and power. Their success isn't just about winning elections. It's about proving that politics can be something more than a game for the elite. It can be a real tool for change when it's in the hands of people who care deeply about their communities.

Historical Significance

Grassroots candidates disrupting political norms isn't a new phenomenon in Canada. It's been happening for as long as people have had the courage to challenge the status quo. These moments stand out because they show what's possible when communities rally behind someone who represents their values, rather than the interests of the political elite. They remind us that the power in democracy ultimately rests with the people, even if it doesn't always feel that way.

One of the earliest examples comes from the prairie provinces in the early 20th century. Farmers, tired of being ignored by traditional political parties, formed their own movements to address issues like fair grain pricing, rural infrastructure, and credit access. These movements, like the United Farmers of Alberta, didn't just make noise—they won elections. In Alberta, the United Farmers formed a government in 1921. What made this particularly significant wasn't just that they won but that they did it without the kind of centralized party structure that dominated politics at the time. Their success was rooted in local organizing, cooperative efforts, and a clear focus on issues that mattered to their communities.

The rise of the Co-operative Commonwealth Federation, or CCF, in the 1930s is another key moment. This was a party born out of grassroots organizing among farmers, labour unions, and social activists. At a time when the Great Depression had devastated much of the country, the CCF offered a bold vision for change, including policies that would eventually shape Canada's social safety net. Their victory in Saskatchewan in

1944, under Tommy Douglas, marked the first time a socialist government was elected in North America. It wasn't just a win for the CCF. It was a turning point in Canadian politics, showing that grassroots movements could not only disrupt but redefine political norms.

Indigenous activism has also played a powerful role in Canadian grassroots politics. The 1960s and 70s saw Indigenous leaders pushing back against government policies that ignored their rights and voices. Leaders like George Manuel, who helped found the National Indian Brotherhood (now the Assembly of First Nations), worked tirelessly to organize and advocate for Indigenous sovereignty and self-determination. While these efforts weren't tied to electoral politics in the traditional sense, they disrupted political norms by forcing governments to address issues they had long ignored. The ripple effects of these movements are still felt today, as Indigenous candidates and activists continue to shape the political landscape.

More recently, Jody Wilson-Raybould's decision to run as an independent in 2019 is a modern example of grassroots disruption. After being removed from the Liberal cabinet, she chose to take her fight directly to the voters in her Vancouver-Granville riding. Running without party support, she built a campaign based on her reputation, values, and connections to her community. Her victory sent a clear message that voters were willing to support candidates who stood for integrity over party loyalty. It was a reminder that even in a system dominated by political parties, there's still room for individuals to break through.

These moments in history share a common thread. Grassroots candidates and movements succeed when they tap into a sense of frustration or urgency in their communities. They don't just run campaigns. They offer an alternative to politics as usual. These disruptions aren't always easy or smooth, but they are necessary. They challenge us to rethink what representation means and who gets to have a say in shaping the future. Looking at these examples, it's clear that grassroots politics has always been an essential part of Canada's democratic fabric. It's not just about winning elections. It's about changing the conversation and proving that political power doesn't always have to flow from the top down.

What Distinguishes Grassroots Candidates

Grassroots candidates stand out because they challenge the usual way politics works. They don't have the same playbook as traditional or party-backed candidates. Instead of relying on political machines, deep pockets, or flashy endorsements, they focus on building genuine connections with the people they want to represent. What makes them unique isn't just where they get their support—it's how they run their campaigns, who they're accountable to, and the priorities they bring to the table.

The biggest difference between grassroots candidates and their party-backed counterparts is their independence. Traditional candidates often benefit from party infrastructure, like fundraising networks, campaign staff, and pre-approved talking points. While this support makes things easier, it comes with strings attached. Party candidates are expected to toe the line on party policies, even if those policies don't match what their local constituents need. Grassroots candidates, on the other hand, answer directly to the people in their communities. They're not bound by party politics, which gives them more freedom to focus on what matters most to the voters they represent.

Another defining characteristic is how grassroots candidates fund their campaigns. Big-money donors and corporate sponsorships aren't part of the equation. Instead, they rely on small-dollar donations from individuals. These contributions aren't just financial; they're symbolic. When someone donates

$10 or $20 to a grassroots campaign, they're not just handing over money. They're buying into a vision and a relationship. This kind of funding makes grassroots candidates less beholden to outside interests and more focused on the people who supported them. It also levels the playing field in a way that's refreshing in a system that often feels dominated by those with the deepest pockets.

Grassroots campaigns are also defined by their approach to voter outreach. Traditional candidates tend to rely on polished marketing and professional campaign teams. Grassroots candidates, by contrast, are more likely to knock on doors themselves, hold small community events, and have one-on-one conversations with voters. These campaigns are scrappy and personal. It's not about glossy brochures or perfectly scripted speeches. It's about showing up, listening, and building trust. Voters can sense when someone is genuinely invested in their community, and grassroots candidates rely on that authenticity to win support.

Community involvement is another hallmark of grassroots candidates. They aren't parachuted into constituencies or handed nominations by party executives. They come from the places they hope to represent. They know the challenges their neighbours face because they've lived them too. This connection to the community gives grassroots candidates a credibility that traditional candidates often struggle to match. They don't need to convince people that they care about local issues—they've already proven it through their actions, long before their names appeared on a ballot.

Grassroots candidates also tend to have a more inclusive approach to building their campaigns. Because they don't have the backing of large organizations, they rely heavily on volunteers. These are people who believe in the candidate and want to help, whether it's by making phone calls, canvassing, or organizing events. This kind of grassroots organizing creates a sense of shared ownership over the campaign. It's not just the candidate's vision—it's the community's vision.

What ties all of these characteristics together is a focus on people. Grassroots candidates prioritize the voices and needs of the people they represent above all else. They don't get bogged down by political games or bureaucratic red tape. They're not trying to climb a party ladder or position themselves for a future cabinet post. Their goals are simpler and more grounded. They want to serve their communities and make a real difference in people's lives. It's this focus on the local and the personal that makes grassroots candidates stand out in a political landscape that often feels disconnected from everyday concerns.

What Distinguishes Grassroots Parties

Grassroots parties are a completely different breed compared to traditional political parties. At their core, grassroots parties are built from the ground up. They prioritize community involvement, local decision-making, and a genuine connection with the people they aim to represent. This is a stark contrast to traditional parties, which often operate in a top-down manner, with decisions made by a centralized leadership and handed down to local chapters or candidates.

The foundation of grassroots parties is their commitment to democratic participation. Traditional parties tend to have tightly controlled nomination processes, policies crafted by party executives, and a strong focus on maintaining party unity. Grassroots parties take the opposite approach. They encourage open discussions, welcome a wide range of voices, and prioritize input from their members. This makes their decision-making more inclusive, even if it's sometimes messy. For grassroots parties, the process matters as much as the outcomes. They value transparency and accountability because they know that their legitimacy depends on it.

One of the most noticeable differences is how grassroots parties approach funding. Traditional parties often rely on large donors, corporate contributions, and a professionalized fundraising apparatus. Grassroots parties, on the other hand, stick to small-dollar donations from individuals. This funding model has a deeper significance than just dollars and cents. It's about ensuring that the party isn't beholden to any single interest group. When the financial backbone of a party comes from ordinary people chipping in what they can, it reinforces the party's accountability to those individuals rather than outside influencers.

Grassroots parties also approach policy-making in a way that feels much more organic. Instead of relying on think tanks or consultants, they tend to draw ideas directly from their members and communities. This means their platforms often reflect a bottom-up perspective, focusing on local issues or systemic changes that resonate with the people who support them. It's not uncommon for grassroots parties to hold public meetings or consultations to develop their policies. This creates a sense of shared ownership over the party's goals, which is something traditional parties rarely achieve.

Organizational structure is another area where grassroots parties set themselves apart. Traditional parties operate like well-oiled machines, with clear hierarchies and professional staff running the show. Grassroots parties are more fluid and decentralized. Volunteers often take on key roles, and decision-making is more collaborative. This can make them seem less polished, but it also allows them to adapt quickly to changing circumstances or new opportunities. Their flexibility and willingness to experiment give them an edge when it comes to connecting with people in unconventional ways.

Grassroots parties are also defined by their local focus. Traditional parties often field candidates who align with the national agenda, regardless of how well those priorities fit with local needs. Grassroots parties flip that script. They start with what matters in their communities and work outward from there. This local-first approach makes them more relevant to voters who feel left behind by national politics. When people see a party fighting for the same things they care about in their neighbourhoods, it builds trust and loyalty that can be hard for traditional parties to replicate.

Another key characteristic is their independence. Traditional parties often work within a well-established political framework, forming alliances, cutting deals, and jockeying for position within the system. Grassroots parties are less constrained by these expectations. They're not afraid to challenge the system itself, whether that means calling out unfair practices, advocating for electoral reform, or questioning the status quo. This outsider status is both a challenge and an advantage. It makes it harder for them to gain traction, but it also allows them to appeal to voters who are tired of business as usual.

What really sets grassroots parties apart, though, is their focus on people over politics. Traditional parties often seem more concerned with winning power than with making a difference. Grassroots parties are driven by a desire to bring about meaningful change, even if that means taking risks or working outside the usual channels. Their approach is more personal, more connected, and ultimately more reflective of the communities they represent.

G rassroots movements have been shaping Canadian politics for generations. They didn't emerge in a vacuum but grew out of frustration and the need for change. These movements were born from people feeling ignored by traditional power structures, whether they were farmers trying to make a living, workers fighting for fair treatment, or Indigenous communities demanding justice. Each of these movements played a significant role in pushing Canada's political landscape toward something more inclusive, even when the odds were stacked against them.

Farmers' movements were some of the earliest examples of grassroots organizing in Canada. At the turn of the 20th century, many farmers felt abandoned by the government and exploited by big businesses, particularly the railways and grain companies. They were being squeezed from every side and had little political representation. Out of this frustration came the United Farmers of Ontario, Alberta, and Manitoba. These weren't just advocacy groups; they became political forces. In Alberta, the United Farmers even formed the provincial government in the 1920s. What made these movements so powerful was their ability to unite people around shared struggles. They created cooperatives, formed alliances, and showed that farmers could organize as effectively as the big players they were up against.

Labour unions followed a similar path. Industrialization brought jobs, but it also brought exploitation, long hours, and unsafe conditions. Workers didn't have a seat at the table, so they built their own. The labour movement in Canada gained momentum in the late 19th and early 20th centuries with organizations like the Trades and Labor Congress of Canada and the rise of strikes that challenged the status quo. The Winnipeg General Strike of 1919 was a turning point. Over 30,000 workers walked off the job, demanding better wages and working conditions. It was a bold statement of solidarity and a clear message to those in power. While the strike didn't achieve all its goals, it galvanized the labour movement and laid the groundwork for political action. The Cooperative Commonwealth Federation, which later became the New Democratic Party, had its roots in these labour struggles, showing how grassroots activism could evolve into lasting political influence.

Indigenous activism has always been a critical part of Canada's grassroots history, even if it wasn't always recognized as such. Long before settlers arrived, Indigenous communities had systems of governance and ways of advocating for their rights. When those rights were stripped away through colonization, Indigenous people found new ways to resist. In the 20th century, leaders like Frederick Loft, who founded the League of Indians of Canada in 1919, began organizing for Indigenous rights on a national level. This early work laid the foundation for later movements like the Red Power movement in the 1960s and 70s, which drew attention to issues like land rights, sovereignty, and systemic racism. Indigenous activism has always been deeply grassroots, driven by local communities and elders while connecting to broader networks of resistance.

Each of these movements, farmers, labour unions, and Indigenous activism, was about more than just the issues at hand. They were about challenging the idea that power should only rest with the few. They showed that when ordinary people come together, they can change the political conversation. These grassroots efforts didn't just demand a seat at the table; they often built their own tables and invited others to join. Looking back at these movements, it's clear that they weren't just moments in history. They were part of an ongoing effort to make Canadian politics more reflective of the people who live here.

The Challenges Of Grassroots Campaigns

Grassroots campaigns face a long list of challenges that make their uphill battle even steeper. These campaigns are built on passion and community, but they often have to work twice as hard as their well-funded, party-backed opponents. Limited funding, restricted access to media, and institutional biases are some of the biggest hurdles they deal with. These obstacles don't just make things inconvenient; they fundamentally shape the way grassroots campaigns operate and what they have to overcome to succeed.

Funding is the most obvious and immediate challenge. Grassroots candidates don't rely on corporate sponsorships or deep-pocketed donors. They turn to their communities for small-dollar donations. While this approach aligns with their values, it's also a significant disadvantage in a political system where money often equals influence. Traditional candidates have the resources to blanket their constituencies with ads, pay for professional staff, and hold large-scale events. Grassroots campaigns operate on shoestring budgets, which means they have to be more creative. They rely on volunteers and prioritize direct engagement with voters. This can be a strength in terms of building authentic connections, but it's no match for the sheer reach that big money can buy.

Media access is another major barrier. Traditional candidates have the backing of established parties, which often guarantees them a certain level of coverage. Party leaders hold press conferences that get national attention, and their candidates benefit from the trickle-down effect. Grassroots candidates don't have that luxury. They often struggle to get noticed by mainstream media, which tends to focus on the big players in any election. Without that coverage, it's hard to get their message out to a broader audience. Social media has levelled the playing field somewhat, but it's not a perfect substitute. Building a social media presence takes time, strategy, and, ironically, sometimes money. Even with a strong online presence, grassroots candidates still face the challenge of breaking through the noise.

Institutional biases are another significant obstacle. The political system in Canada wasn't designed with grassroots candidates in mind. Party-backed candidates benefit from the infrastructure of their parties, from nomination processes to election-day logistics. Independent or grassroots candidates have to figure all of this out on their own. The electoral system itself, with its first-past-the-post structure, tends to favour well-established parties. Winning as a grassroots candidate often means unseating someone who has the advantage of party resources and name recognition. On top of that, there's often skepticism from voters, who may see grassroots candidates as underdogs or outsiders. While some people find that appealing, others view it as a disadvantage, worrying that these candidates lack the experience or connections to be effective.

There's also a cultural bias in how politics is perceived. Traditional candidates often come with polished resumes, professional campaigns, and an air of legitimacy that grassroots candidates might struggle to project. The system rewards those who play by its rules, and grassroots candidates, by their very nature, are trying to rewrite those rules. This makes them disruptive, which can be a selling point for some voters but a red flag for others who prefer stability or familiarity.

Grassroots campaigns also have to work harder to build trust. Traditional candidates benefit from the institutional credibility of their parties, even if that credibility is sometimes misplaced. Grassroots candidates don't have that automatic legitimacy. They have to earn every vote by proving themselves to their communities. This means countless hours spent at community events, knocking on doors, and having one-on-one conversations. It's rewarding work, but it's also exhausting, especially when resources are limited and the clock is ticking.

These challenges aren't insurmountable, but they force grassroots campaigns to be resourceful and resilient. They have to stretch every dollar, amplify every opportunity for exposure, and push back against a system that often feels stacked against them. While the barriers are real and daunting, they also highlight the courage and determination it takes to run a grassroots campaign in the first place.

A significant portion of voters are not rational voters, and that's simply a fact of politics. Many people aren't all that interested in politics or the nuances of policy. They don't have the time or the inclination to dive deep into every candidate's platform or to weigh the pros and cons of different approaches to governance. For most, voting is a lot more about gut feeling than it is about detailed analysis. They want to pick a candidate who they think will improve their lives, and that choice is often made based on impressions, emotions, or what they hear from friends, family, or media. It's not about looking at every issue and carefully considering every detail. For many voters, it's about finding someone who speaks to their concerns and makes them feel like they matter.

In many cases, voters will simply choose the candidate who says the things they want to hear. This is where the challenge for grassroots candidates comes in. They are often up against candidates who have big corporate backing or established party structures, which can give them the resources to push messages that sound nice on the surface but may not have any real substance behind them. These so-called populist leaders know that a lot of voters will simply latch onto whatever promises sound good, even if those promises are unrealistic or built on lies. It's not about what's best for the community in the long run; it's about saying the things that will make voters feel heard in the short term. It's easy to say, "I'll lower taxes," "I'll create jobs," or "I'll fix the economy," without explaining how or why. A lot of voters, especially those who are disengaged or uninformed, won't ask questions. They'll just hear what they want to hear and believe it.

However, grassroots candidates also tap into a kind of populism, though it's different from the hollow promises of more traditional populist figures. Grassroots platforms often focus on the issues that matter most to everyday people—things like affordable housing, better healthcare, fair wages, and a living wage. These candidates understand that in order to win over voters, they need to communicate that they will make life better for everyone. But unlike the populists who might promise the moon with no plan to deliver, grassroots candidates usually have more concrete, community-focused platforms. Their message is grounded in the real needs of the people, and their campaigns often reflect a genuine desire to make change from the ground up, not from a top-down perspective.

It's in the best interest of grassroots candidates and parties to communicate to voters in whatever way they can that they will make everyone's lives better. Whether it's through community events, social media outreach, or old-fashioned door-to-door campaigning, these candidates need to build trust and make it clear that they are on the side of the people. They want voters to see them as someone who understands their struggles and has the drive to make meaningful changes. The challenge is that for many voters, the decision is made based on impressions or what they hear in the media, not necessarily on a detailed understanding of policies or past performance. This means that grassroots candidates have to work harder to break through the noise of traditional party politics and show that they're the ones who can make a real difference.

In the end, it's all about making that connection with the voter. Grassroots candidates can't always rely on the same financial backing or media exposure as their more established competitors. What they do have is the ability to connect with voters on a personal level, to speak to their concerns and show that they are not just another politician looking to secure power for personal gain. They can tap into the populist spirit that drives many voters, but they do so with a message that is rooted in sincerity and a true desire to improve lives, not just win votes. They understand that for a lot of voters, the decision is emotional, not intellectual. And that's why they focus on being relatable, accessible, and clear about their intentions.

Recruiting Candidates

G rassroots parties can benefit greatly by using strategies similar to those employed by larger parties when it comes to recruiting candidates. While major parties have extensive networks and resources for candidate recruitment, grassroots movements can adopt many of the same approaches to ensure they have strong, capable candidates to run in elections. These strategies centre on identifying and empowering individuals who are well-suited to represent their communities and who can inspire others to join the movement.

One key approach used by major parties is identifying potential candidates who already have a track record of involvement in their communities. This often includes people who have experience in local activism, volunteer work, or have held leadership positions in community organizations. These individuals tend to have the networks and local support that make them natural fits for running for office. For grassroots candidates, recruiting is similarly about finding people who are already connected to the issues that matter most to the community. By attending community meetings, connecting with local organizations, and becoming involved in advocacy efforts, grassroots movements can identify potential candidates who are passionate and already respected by their peers. These individuals can then be approached and encouraged to take on a leadership role within the campaign.

Another method used by large parties to recruit candidates is offering training and guidance. New candidates often need help navigating the complexities of running a campaign, and major parties provide the necessary support, from fundraising advice to campaign management tips. While grassroots movements might not have the same level of institutional support, they can still make use of available resources to train potential candidates. Grassroots organizations can connect with local political groups, community leaders, or nonprofits that offer workshops or guidance for candidates, ensuring that new recruits are prepared for the challenges of running for office. These resources help potential candidates feel confident in their decision to step forward and run.

Building coalitions is another essential part of candidate recruitment for major parties, and it's something grassroots candidates can also use to their advantage. Large parties create coalitions by bringing together a range of interest groups, which provides both a support network and a potential pool of candidates. Grassroots movements can similarly reach out to various community organizations and groups, whether labour unions, environmental groups, or local activists, to identify individuals who are passionate about specific issues and could represent these concerns in the political sphere. By aligning with these organizations and gaining their support, grassroots candidates can expand their pool of potential recruits and build a team that is committed to representing the diverse interests of the community.

Successful parties also make use of a clear, unified message that attracts new candidates. For grassroots movements, having a clear, resonant message is essential for recruiting individuals who are committed to fighting for the same values and goals. Grassroots movements can attract candidates who believe in the cause and who are motivated by a desire to create positive change. By focusing on key issues, whether healthcare, housing, or education, grassroots movements can recruit candidates who are not only passionate about those issues but who also have the experience and credibility to speak on them. This unified message helps potential candidates see the importance of running and gives them the confidence to step forward.

Another tactic used by major parties to recruit candidates is holding informational meetings or outreach events. These gatherings give prospective candidates a chance to learn more about what running for office involves, and they often serve as a space for individuals to ask questions and decide if they are ready to commit. Grassroots movements can do the same by hosting community events where potential candidates can learn more about the campaign, meet current leaders, and understand what the role would involve. These meetings allow grassroots movements to build personal connections with potential candidates, answer their questions, and offer encouragement for them to run.

Additionally, grassroots movements can also use social media and digital tools to identify and recruit candidates. While major parties rely on established media networks to spread their recruitment efforts, grassroots campaigns can leverage the power of social media platforms to reach a broader audience. Online platforms make it easier to connect with potential candidates who might not otherwise be on the radar. By creating a strong online presence, grassroots movements can promote opportunities to get involved, call for new candidates, and create spaces for people to express their interest in running.

Recruiting candidates within grassroots campaigns doesn't necessarily require large amounts of money or resources. It's about identifying people who are passionate, motivated, and connected to their communities. By using these strategies, grassroots movements can bring together individuals who are ready to step up and make a difference, even without the backing of major parties. When done effectively, this recruitment process helps ensure that the campaign is strong, diverse, and has the right people in place to succeed.

The Hard Work

Running a grassroots campaign in Canada is rarely a smooth ride. Most of the time, it's an uphill battle, one that requires a lot of grit and determination. Unlike the well-funded, heavily resourced campaigns of larger political parties, grassroots candidates often start with very little. The candidate has to roll up their sleeves and get to work, often with limited financial backing and a much smaller team. This means they can't just rely on expensive ads or slick promotional campaigns to get their message out. Instead, they have to rely on personal connections, community engagement, and the tireless efforts of volunteers who believe in their vision.

A huge part of the challenge comes from inspiring and maintaining the enthusiasm of those volunteers. These individuals are usually motivated by a sense of purpose and the belief that they can make a real difference, but they are also often juggling their personal lives with this extra commitment. The candidate has to be someone who can energize their team, make them feel valued, and remind them of the bigger picture when the going gets tough. It's easy for people to get discouraged when things aren't moving as quickly as they'd hoped or when they're faced with setbacks. The candidate has to keep that spark alive, showing the team that their efforts, no matter how small they might seem, are contributing to something larger than themselves.

Grassroots campaigns also face logistical hurdles that larger campaigns don't usually have to contend with. They don't have the big budget to hire staff for every aspect of the campaign.

The candidate and their team might be doing everything from knocking on doors, organizing events, and managing social media accounts to fundraising and planning strategy. It can be exhausting, especially when the candidate has to balance these responsibilities with the demands of daily life. Often, the candidate will find themselves putting in long hours, sacrificing personal time, and pushing themselves beyond their limits. And even with all this hard work, there's no guarantee that they'll win the election. That's a tough reality for many grassroots candidates to face. But for those who believe in what they're doing and who are committed to serving their community, the struggle becomes a testament to their resolve.

There's also the emotional toll that can come with running a campaign. The candidate is putting themselves out there, subjecting themselves to public scrutiny, criticism, and sometimes even personal attacks. They're asking people to trust them, to believe in their vision for change, but not everyone will support them. This can be hard to deal with, especially when you're up against powerful political forces. A grassroots candidate has to be able to maintain their confidence, even when the odds seem stacked against them, and keep pushing forward. There are times when they might feel like giving up, when the challenges seem insurmountable, but those are the moments that truly test their commitment.

Despite all the hurdles, there's something uniquely rewarding about grassroots campaigns. When you're out there talking to voters, hearing their concerns, and rallying together with people who believe in your cause, it can feel incredibly powerful. The sense of community and shared purpose is something that larger campaigns can't always replicate. In the end, the hard work, the long hours, the sacrifices, and the emotional strain can all be worth it when you see that the effort has made a real impact.

Candidate Confidence And Authenticity

Candidate confidence and authenticity are crucial when it comes to electability. Voters want to see someone who genuinely believes in their message and isn't afraid to stand up for what they believe in. The ability to speak to voters with sincerity, to make them feel that the candidate truly understands their struggles and is there to represent their interests, is what often separates grassroots candidates from their more polished, establishment-backed counterparts. It's not just about presenting a set of well-rehearsed talking points. It's about showing that the candidate is real, grounded in the community, and committed to making a difference for the everyday person.

When a candidate exudes confidence, it's not about arrogance. It's about a quiet assurance that they are the right person for the job and that their vision for the future is rooted in what people actually need, not in what's most politically expedient. That kind of confidence is infectious. When voters see a candidate who stands tall, speaks with conviction, and remains steady in their beliefs, it creates a sense of trust. Voters feel like they're not being sold a product or being talked down to. They feel like they're speaking to someone who's one of them, someone who understands the struggles of the average person and is willing to fight for those who have been left behind by the establishment.

Authenticity plays a huge role in this. People are savvy. They know when a candidate is putting on a show or trying to sell them an image that doesn't line up with reality. What makes a grassroots candidate stand out is their ability to be real, to show that they aren't just another politician trying to make deals in the background or appease special interests. They are people who are genuinely interested in what the voters have to say and who take their concerns seriously. Authenticity can't be manufactured. It's something that comes from consistently living out the values the candidate claims to stand for, and it's something that resonates deeply with voters.

A candidate who communicates with authenticity creates an impression of honesty. In a political climate where many voters feel disillusioned by the lack of transparency in government, honesty becomes a valuable commodity. When voters believe that a candidate is being honest with them, when they feel like the candidate isn't hiding anything or sugarcoating the truth, they are more likely to trust that person with their vote. This trust doesn't happen overnight, but it's built through consistent action, by staying true to the values that originally brought the candidate into the race, and by being open about their intentions.

Voters are also drawn to candidates who prioritize their interests over the interests of the wealthy, the corporations, or other elite groups. When a grassroots candidate makes it clear that they will fight for the regular folk, that they aren't beholden to powerful lobbyists or donors, it resonates with people who feel like they've been ignored by the political establishment. It's not just about saying the right things. It's about showing, through actions and words, that the candidate's priorities lie with the people who need help the most. The sense that a candidate will stand up for them, that they won't back down in the face of pressure from powerful forces, gives voters a sense of hope that things can actually change.

In a world where politics often feels like a game played by a small, disconnected elite, grassroots candidates who project confidence and authenticity offer a refreshing change. They speak to the voters in ways that cut through the noise of political gamesmanship and focus on what really matters: the well-being of the people. Their electability is not just about their policies, but about the way they connect with their constituents and the impression they leave. When a candidate comes across as someone who is truly invested in the community and who can be trusted to put the voters' interests first, it makes all the difference in whether they win or lose.

The Grassroots Challenge

Grassroots parties and candidates in Canada face a challenge that is both unique and difficult to overcome. Unlike the larger parties, which can rely on a top-down approach with a unified platform designed to appeal to broad national interests, grassroots candidates need to make a personal connection with voters. This is crucial for building trust and demonstrating that the candidate genuinely understands and cares about the local issues that matter most to their community. A broad, one-size-fits-all platform simply won't work for grassroots candidates who need to show they are in touch with the unique needs of the people they aim to represent. For a grassroots party to succeed, it has to strike a balance between a unified, cohesive platform and the diverse priorities of individual candidates.

Rather than trying to create a single, all-encompassing platform that seeks to cover every issue from coast to coast, a grassroots party should focus on showcasing how its diverse candidates come together for common causes. Each candidate represents a different part of the community, each with their own experiences and priorities. Some might focus on environmental issues, others on healthcare, while others might be more concerned with housing or education. The strength of a grassroots movement lies in its ability to unite these varied concerns under a common banner that highlights shared values. The party platform should reflect this diversity, but it should also make clear where the common ground lies. What brings these candidates together is their shared commitment to improving the lives of those in their local communities, even if the specific issues they prioritize differ.

One of the most powerful ways a grassroots party can create an impression of authenticity and relatability is by allowing its candidates to differentiate themselves on the issues that matter most to their specific constituents. This doesn't mean that the party needs to splinter into factions or that candidates should promote radically different ideas. Instead, it means recognizing that each community has unique challenges, and the candidates are the best ones to understand and address those challenges. By empowering candidates to speak to the local issues they care about, the party can show that it's not just about selling a generic set of policies to the masses. Rather, it's about understanding the needs of each community and trusting the candidates to be the best advocates for those needs. This approach allows the grassroots party to look more like a reflection of real people with real concerns, rather than a distant, top-down political machine.

To further strengthen their position, grassroots candidates should be encouraged to highlight the differences in their platforms, especially when it comes to local issues. This doesn't mean that the party's platform should be a free-for-all where anything goes. Instead, it's about recognizing that local communities have different needs, and a grassroots movement can be more flexible in addressing these needs than larger parties. For example, a candidate in a rural area might prioritize agricultural policies or infrastructure improvements, while a candidate in a major urban centre might focus more on housing, transit, or environmental policies. A national party might struggle to address these specific concerns in detail, but a grassroots candidate can give a much-needed voice to these local issues. This approach helps distinguish grassroots candidates from the traditional parties, whose platforms often struggle to address the diversity of local needs across the country.

At the same time, this local emphasis shouldn't mean a disjointed or chaotic platform. A well-designed grassroots platform should still highlight the party's overarching values and goals. It should show that despite the local differences, the party stands united in its commitment to addressing inequality, ensuring access to healthcare, improving education, or whatever other issues are central to the grassroots movement's goals. The diversity in the candidates' platforms should be seen as a strength, not a weakness. It reflects the idea that a strong party isn't one that demands every candidate adhere to a single, rigid set of policies, but rather one that can flex and adapt to the different needs of various communities.

Ultimately, the success of a grassroots party in Canada depends on its ability to connect with voters in a way that is both personal and reflective of local needs. It's about showing that candidates are truly listening to their communities and addressing the issues that matter most to them. While a national platform can certainly offer some guiding principles, the real power of a grassroots movement lies in the ability of its candidates to speak directly to the unique concerns of their constituents. When a grassroots party embraces the diversity of its candidates and allows them to advocate for the issues that matter most to their communities, it becomes a true reflection of the people it aims to represent.

The Grassroots Commitment

To make real strides in an election, a grassroots party in Canada has to craft a message that resonates with regular folks, convincing them that the party will bring about tangible changes that will improve their lives. The challenge here isn't just about offering vague promises. It's about providing a clear and compelling case for why this party is different from all the others and showing how it can truly make life better for everyday Canadians. The first step in achieving this is committing to electoral reform. Without reforming the current system, it will be incredibly difficult for any party, especially a grassroots one, to bring about the kind of changes that would make a meaningful difference. The current political structure often locks out new ideas and creates barriers for smaller, non-establishment parties to have their voices heard in parliament. Electoral reform is not just a nice idea; it's a necessity for making sure that the voices of the people are properly represented and that the political system can actually deliver on the changes that Canadians need.

One of the most pressing issues that a grassroots party can focus on is the affordability crisis. Right now, this is the one issue that directly affects the majority of Canadians. Whether it's the high cost of housing, skyrocketing utility bills, or just the basic challenge of making ends meet, affordability is the issue that is top of mind for most people. A grassroots party that wants to make a real impact will need to make this its central focus, showing voters that it has a plan to address these issues head-on. Promising vague solutions or passing the problem off to future governments just won't cut it. Canadians are tired of waiting for change that never seems to come. If a grassroots party wants to win the trust of the people, it needs to step up and show that it can offer something concrete and meaningful to address the affordability crisis right now.

The next step is ensuring that any policies put forward are purposeful and grounded in evidence. Too often, politicians propose policies that sound good in theory but fail to produce real-world results. Grassroots candidates need to prove that they're different by focusing on evidence-based policy that actually works. This means working with experts, academics, and professionals in various fields to craft policies that are not just well-meaning but actually effective in bringing about the change that is needed. It's not enough to just talk about the problems; solutions need to be based on real data and careful analysis. The party's policies should reflect a clear understanding of the issues and a commitment to using the best available evidence to solve them.

One of the best ways to demonstrate that these policies will work is to take the step of drafting actual legislation. Rather than relying on lofty promises or vague outlines, the party should develop concrete proposals that can hold up under the scrutiny of experts and academics. This isn't just about creating a list of ideas; it's about creating a roadmap for real change. Drafting legislation that addresses the affordability crisis, for example, shows that the party is not just talking about the problem but is serious about solving it. By working with experts to ensure that these proposals are realistic and feasible, the party can demonstrate its commitment to effective, evidence-based solutions. Moreover, these proposals give the public something tangible to rally behind. Instead of just hearing vague rhetoric about change, voters will have a clear understanding of what the party plans to do and how it plans to get there.

Having draft legislation that can be analyzed and critiqued by experts serves another important purpose: it helps build credibility. For a grassroots party to succeed, it needs to establish trust with the public. Drafting real policies that are backed by experts shows voters that the party isn't just saying what they think people want to hear. It's showing that they're willing to put in the work and develop meaningful, well-thought-out solutions. This is especially important in a political climate where people are increasingly skeptical of promises that never seem to come to fruition. When voters see that a grassroots party has a well-developed, evidence-based plan for addressing the affordability crisis and other issues, it can help shift the narrative from being seen as an outsider or underdog to being seen as a credible and effective alternative to the established parties.

Ultimately, a grassroots party that wants to make major gains in an election has to commit to a vision of real change that will resonate with regular people. Electoral reform is the foundation for making sure that the party's voice is heard in parliament, and the affordability crisis should be the party's central focus. But it's not enough to just promise change. A grassroots party needs to back up its promises with concrete, evidence-based policies that can be analyzed and scrutinized by experts. Drafting real legislation is the best way to show that the party is serious about making those changes a reality. In the end, it's about demonstrating to voters that this party is ready and capable of bringing about the changes they've been waiting for.

Door-To-Door Canvassing

Door-to-door canvassing has remained one of the most powerful tools in a grassroots political campaign. While technology has changed how campaigns reach voters, nothing beats the personal connection of knocking on someone's door and introducing them to a candidate face-to-face. The message is simple: this is our candidate, this is why they're great, and we want you to be a part of this movement. The interaction is brief, but it's meaningful. The goal is not to try and gauge who is going to vote for you right then and there. It's not about identifying voter intent or trying to convince someone on the spot. It's about making a personal connection, showing up, and letting people know that a candidate is actively engaging with their community.

This approach works because it's authentic. In a world where people feel disconnected from the political process, someone showing up at their door represents a real effort. It's not a paid political consultant making a call or an automated message. It's a person who cares enough about the issues to show up and talk to them directly. It doesn't matter if the person at the door is already set in their political views or not interested in volunteering. The point is that the candidate's campaign is there, showing their commitment to being accessible and present.

One of the best parts of this strategy is that it doesn't require huge financial backing. You don't need a massive budget to buy expensive ads or media placements. What you need is a network of volunteers who are willing to give their time to knock on doors and have those simple, respectful conversations. When it's done right, it feels less like a pitch and more like a genuine effort to connect with people. A candidate is not asking for anything other than the opportunity to be heard, and it's up to the individual whether they want to get involved further, whether by taking a lawn sign or offering to volunteer.

The beauty of door-to-door canvassing is its accessibility. It brings politics into people's homes in a way that's personal and human. It's not just a one-way communication where the campaign dumps information on the voter. It opens up a space where voters can express concerns, ask questions, or simply learn about the candidate. It's a conversation, not an interrogation. And after a few quick questions and sharing the candidate's vision, the canvasser says thank you for your time and moves on to the next door, ensuring that no one feels pressured or overwhelmed.

Even if people do not immediately volunteer or take a lawn sign, the impact of these interactions is long-lasting. People remember who showed up at their door, and that's a powerful thing. It makes a campaign feel more genuine and less transactional. Over time, the candidate becomes a part of the community fabric, not just a name on a ballot. This type of canvassing works because it's rooted in real human connection. The simplicity and authenticity are what allow grassroots candidates to thrive even without the deep pockets or media dominance that larger, party-backed candidates often enjoy. When a candidate is truly connected to the community, it shows in every knock on the door.

Voter outreach is absolutely essential for grassroots candidates. The key to a successful grassroots campaign is ensuring that the candidate is not just a name on a ballot, but a real presence in the community. Grassroots candidates may not have the same resources as their party-backed counterparts, but they make up for it with their accessibility and willingness to engage directly with voters. It's about being visible, approachable, and invested in the concerns of the people. When candidates are out in the community, attending public events, hosting "meet the candidate" gatherings, or simply volunteering their time for public service, they send a clear message that they are present and genuinely care about the issues that affect people's lives.

These types of interactions allow voters to see the candidate as a person, not just a politician. When candidates show up at community events, whether it's a neighbourhood cleanup, a town hall, or a local festival, they are not only making themselves accessible but also demonstrating that they understand the community's needs. These events provide voters with the chance to talk directly to the candidate, ask questions, and share their concerns. This kind of direct, personal engagement fosters a connection that goes beyond campaign slogans or promises. It builds trust.

When a candidate takes the time to meet with voters face-to-face, it allows them to convey a sense of authenticity. The more a candidate is seen in the community, the more they build the impression that they are in touch with what people are going through. This also allows the candidate to show competence, to demonstrate that they understand the issues at hand and that they have practical solutions. It's one thing to hear a candidate speak at a rally or on TV, but it's something entirely different to have a conversation with them in person, where they can listen to your concerns and respond thoughtfully.

Grassroots candidates can also inspire confidence in their ability to lead by showing up consistently and engaging with voters in ways that make them feel valued. It's not about just getting votes; it's about building a relationship with the community. Voters want to know that the candidate they are supporting is not just another political figure who will disappear after the election. They want to know that the person they are voting for will continue to be present, that they will listen, and that they will act in the best interest of the people they represent. Grassroots candidates who are actively involved in public service or who take part in community-building activities prove that they are committed to serving others, not just seeking power.

When a candidate is consistently visible and engaged, it cultivates the perception that they are competent, that they know what they are doing, and that they can be trusted to follow through on their promises. Even without the financial backing of larger parties, these candidates are able to create a strong, positive impression simply by showing up and putting in the effort to connect with voters. In a way, it becomes a self-fulfilling prophecy. The more a candidate connects with people and demonstrates their dedication to the community, the more the community feels that they are the right choice. Voter outreach helps reinforce the idea that the candidate is not only competent but also someone who will truly represent the interests of the people. This process builds a sense of confidence and trust that is vital for a grassroots campaign's success.

Volunteer Mobilization

Volunteer mobilization is at the heart of any successful grassroots campaign. It's one of the key ingredients that allow these candidates to compete with the big parties that often have access to far more resources. Volunteers bring something that money can't buy: enthusiasm and a sense of community. They believe in the cause, and they're willing to put in the hard work to make it happen. This kind of energy is contagious and can have a huge impact on a campaign. Grassroots candidates rely on this network to get their message out, knock on doors, distribute signs, organize events, and even fundraise. The success of these efforts often hinges on the willingness of volunteers to donate their time and energy because, without them, many campaigns would struggle to reach the voters they need to.

In many ways, the volunteer network becomes the backbone of the campaign. These are the people who are out there every day, talking to neighbours, answering questions, and building relationships. They help spread the word in a way that's both personal and effective. It's one thing to see an ad on TV or hear a politician's soundbite on the radio, but when someone you know personally knocks on your door or speaks to you at a local event, it's much more powerful. Volunteers are the ones who build those connections. They aren't just advocating for a political platform; they're spreading the candidate's message in a way that feels authentic and sincere. Their connection to the community gives the campaign a grassroots, local flavour that the major parties often can't replicate.

One of the most important roles that volunteers play is in expanding the candidate's reach. They help spread the word in ways that go beyond traditional advertising. Whether it's sharing a candidate's social media posts, organizing meetups, or simply talking to people in their own circles, volunteers are the amplifiers of a campaign's message. The more they engage, the more they bring in new supporters. What's great about volunteer mobilization is that it taps into the power of word-of-mouth, which is still one of the most effective forms of communication. People trust the opinions of friends, family, and colleagues more than they do the polished, scripted messages of politicians. Volunteers bring that personal touch, making the campaign feel less like a top-down operation and more like a movement that's built from the ground up.

It's not just about helping out with the logistics of the campaign, though. Volunteers are also vital for building momentum. Enthusiastic volunteers can inspire others to get involved, creating a ripple effect that builds excitement and energy. Their belief in the candidate and the cause can act as a magnet for more people to join in. When a candidate's team is full of passionate volunteers, it sends a message to the electorate that this campaign is something worth paying attention to. The more people see that the candidate has strong community support, the more likely they are to consider getting involved themselves or voting for the candidate. This kind of momentum is what helps grassroots campaigns take off. It starts with a few dedicated people, but as more people join in, the energy snowballs, and the campaign gains real traction.

It's also worth noting that volunteers often bring skills and experiences that can benefit a campaign in ways that go beyond just knocking on doors or making phone calls. Many volunteers have professional backgrounds that can contribute to the campaign's success. They may have expertise in communications, event planning, or fundraising. They may also have strong ties to local organizations or community groups, which can help the candidate make important connections. The diversity of a volunteer network adds depth to a grassroots campaign, giving it the flexibility to tackle a wide range of challenges. A well-organized volunteer network can handle everything from canvassing to strategic planning to crisis management. Volunteers are often the ones who help fill in the gaps when a campaign is short on resources or manpower.

For grassroots candidates, keeping volunteers motivated and engaged is key. This means offering them more than just the opportunity to help out with the campaign. Successful volunteer programs make people feel like they're part of something bigger. They provide training, recognition, and opportunities for volunteers to develop new skills. They also create a sense of community among volunteers, helping them form lasting connections with others who share their values and beliefs. When volunteers feel appreciated and valued, they're more likely to stay committed to the cause and continue working hard throughout the campaign. This kind of dedication is invaluable and can make a real difference when it comes to turning out voters and achieving success on election day.

Ultimately, the power of volunteer mobilization lies in the collective effort of many people working toward a common goal. It's about creating a movement that feels real, authentic, and rooted in the community. Grassroots campaigns may not have the same financial backing or media exposure as the major parties, but they can build something even more powerful: a network of dedicated, passionate individuals who believe in the candidate and the cause. Volunteers bring that passion to the table, and their energy is what makes grassroots campaigns thrive.

Coalition Building

B uilding a coalition is one of the most important aspects of a grassroots campaign. It's about creating alliances with organizations and individuals who share common values, even if they don't always agree on everything. These partnerships can amplify a campaign's message, increase its reach, and provide resources that would be hard to come by otherwise. Activist groups, environmental organizations, and other civic groups play a key role in these coalitions because they often have a loyal base of supporters who are already passionate about the issues that matter most to the candidate. When a grassroots campaign taps into these groups, it gains access to a network of people who are already motivated and ready to take action.

Environmental groups, for example, are a natural ally for grassroots candidates who prioritize sustainable policies. These organizations already have the infrastructure in place to mobilize voters and raise awareness about environmental issues. By aligning with them, a candidate can gain not only visibility on important issues but also the support of people who care deeply about the environment. This can bring in a demographic that might otherwise be skeptical of mainstream political parties, giving the candidate a broader base of support. Similarly, activist groups that focus on social justice, labour rights, or income inequality can provide a much-needed voice for candidates who want to challenge the status quo and push for meaningful change.

Beyond these more traditional groups, other grassroots candidates and parties can also be valuable allies. These candidates often share similar values and face the same challenges in running a campaign. By coming together, they can pool their resources, share strategies, and provide each other with moral and practical support. Even if the candidates belong to different political parties or movements, the focus can remain on common goals, like achieving policy changes that benefit the public and challenge entrenched power structures. In this way, grassroots candidates can create a united front that shows voters there is a real, viable alternative to the established political parties.

Civic organizations are another group that can bolster a grassroots campaign. These organizations often work directly with local communities, and they have deep roots in areas that grassroots candidates might otherwise struggle to reach. Whether it's through organizing community events, running educational programs, or advocating for local causes, these organizations can provide grassroots candidates with a platform to connect directly with voters. A candidate who partners with these groups can tap into a wealth of local knowledge and expertise that can help them craft policies that truly reflect the needs of the community. These partnerships can also help a candidate gain credibility, as they show a commitment to the issues that matter most to the people they hope to represent.

The beauty of coalition-building in grassroots campaigns is that it's mutually beneficial. When activist groups, environmental organizations, civic groups, and other candidates come together, they all stand to gain from the partnership. The grassroots candidate gets access to a broader network of supporters, while the organizations involved get a chance to influence policy decisions and help push for change. These groups often have a wealth of knowledge about the issues they care about, and they can help a candidate develop a policy platform that reflects the concerns of their communities. This can make the candidate's platform more robust and grounded in real-world issues, which makes it easier to win the support of undecided voters.

Building a coalition also helps grassroots candidates fight back against the enormous advantages of wealthier, more established parties. Major parties often have access to vast amounts of money, media resources, and a well-oiled political machine. For grassroots candidates, these resources are often out of reach. But by building strong alliances with other organizations and candidates, they can level the playing field. The combined power of a coalition can bring visibility, credibility, and momentum to a campaign that might otherwise struggle to be heard. It also sends a message to voters that the candidate is serious about building a broad-based movement that can achieve real, lasting change.

An important aspect of coalition-building is that it helps create a sense of solidarity. When different groups and individuals come together under a common cause, it fosters a sense of unity and shared purpose. This can be powerful in rallying voters who might be feeling disillusioned with the political system. It shows them that change is possible and that there is strength in numbers. It also helps build trust between the candidate and voters. A candidate who is able to unite different groups shows that they are not just focused on winning an election for personal gain, but that they are working to build something bigger than themselves. This message of unity and collaboration can be incredibly appealing to voters who are looking for a candidate they can believe in.

In the end, coalition-building is all about creating a broad, inclusive movement that reflects the diverse interests and concerns of the community. By aligning with activist groups, environmental organizations, other grassroots candidates, and civic groups, a grassroots campaign can build the kind of momentum needed to challenge the established political system. These alliances help expand a candidate's reach, increase their credibility, and provide the resources necessary to run an effective campaign. More importantly, they create a sense of solidarity and purpose that can inspire voters to get involved, take action, and help bring about the change they want to see.

Reaching Out To Unions

When grassroots candidates reach out to unions, they tap into a powerful resource that can help them connect with a large portion of their community. Unions are deeply embedded in Canadian society, with nearly a third of working Canadians belonging to one. These organizations are not just about negotiating better wages and working conditions; they also play a significant role in encouraging their members to engage with the broader community, including political campaigns and elections. This is where grassroots candidates can benefit.

Unions in Canada are much more than just places of work representation. They often have long-standing traditions of political involvement and activism. Many unions run political action committees specifically designed to support the political causes and candidates that align with the interests of their members. These committees work to advocate for policies that benefit workers, like better healthcare, fair wages, and workers' rights, which can create a natural partnership with candidates who prioritize these same issues.

By building relationships with unions, a grassroots candidate can not only gain the support of union members but also benefit from the extensive networks these unions provide. Unions have established trust within their communities and can serve as a bridge to voters who might otherwise be harder to reach. For example, many unions have established channels for communication, from newsletters to social media pages, where they can amplify the candidate's message. This creates a built-in audience for grassroots candidates who may not have the financial resources to invest in large-scale advertising campaigns.

The support from unions can also help candidates with boots-on-the-ground organizing. Many unions encourage their members to take an active role in political campaigns, whether it's through canvassing, attending events, or getting involved in fundraising. This type of grassroots mobilization is invaluable for a candidate looking to increase their visibility and rally support in a community. Unions often have a wide base of volunteers and activists who are passionate about their causes and are ready to channel that energy into supporting candidates who will champion those causes in government.

Union endorsement can also send a strong signal to voters. When a union backs a candidate, it provides a form of validation that can resonate with voters, particularly those in working-class communities. It shows that the candidate is aligned with the interests of everyday people and that they have the support of an organization that fights for the rights and needs of workers. This can help position the candidate as someone who is truly in tune with the concerns of the electorate, and it can also help attract undecided voters who may view union support as a sign of legitimacy.

In a political landscape where corporate interests often dominate, union support provides grassroots candidates with a much-needed counterbalance. It gives them a foothold in local communities, bolstering their campaigns with the kind of infrastructure and network that can turn a good candidate into an electoral force. By connecting with unions and leveraging their resources, grassroots candidates can break through the barriers that might otherwise limit their ability to reach voters and build the kind of community-driven momentum that leads to electoral success.

Indigenous Representation

Indigenous candidates face barriers that others might not. These challenges stem from a long history of under-representation, systemic discrimination, and the lack of access to political power. But while these obstacles are significant, they also create opportunities for candidates to bring fresh perspectives, solutions, and strategies to the table.

Indigenous candidates often face the challenge of overcoming stereotypes and prejudices that are deeply rooted in Canadian society. The history of colonialism has created a situation where Indigenous communities are often viewed through a lens of deficit, where their struggles are seen as problems to be solved rather than a reality to be understood and respected. Grassroots Indigenous candidates must navigate this history and its impact on their communities while also trying to create a narrative that resonates with the broader electorate. They often face skepticism from both their own communities and the larger public, who might not fully understand or appreciate the complexities of Indigenous identity, culture, and issues. This can be especially difficult when trying to run a campaign in a system that is largely designed for those who already have access to political power.

The key to overcoming these challenges is often rooted in authenticity and community connections. Indigenous candidates, more than anyone, need to be seen as real representatives of their people, not just politicians seeking to gain office. They often rely on the strength of their local connections and the trust they have within their communities to help them build support. This authenticity is important, as voters are increasingly tired of seeing candidates who make promises they do not intend to keep. Indigenous candidates can stand out by showing that they are genuinely committed to making a difference in the lives of their communities. By being honest about the challenges they face and the solutions they advocate for, they build trust with voters who are looking for someone they can believe in.

At the same time, Indigenous candidates often have unique strategies that set them apart from other grassroots candidates. One of the most important is the ability to speak directly to issues that impact Indigenous communities in a way that few other candidates can. These include issues like land rights, access to education and healthcare, environmental protections, and cultural preservation. These issues are not just political for Indigenous people; they are deeply personal and tied to their identity and way of life. Indigenous candidates can connect with voters by showing how their own experiences and history give them a unique perspective on these challenges, and by offering solutions that are grounded in the needs and aspirations of Indigenous communities.

A key strategy for Indigenous candidates is also their ability to leverage their cultural knowledge and values. Indigenous communities are often highly engaged in grassroots movements, with many organizations and activists already advocating for change. Indigenous candidates can tap into these movements to build momentum and create a platform that is both reflective of their community's values and resonant with the broader electorate. These candidates can also work to bridge the gap between Indigenous and non-Indigenous voters by framing issues in a way that emphasizes shared values, like respect for the land, the importance of family and community, and the need for social justice. This kind of messaging can attract support from a wide range of voters who might not otherwise engage with Indigenous issues, as it highlights common ground and fosters empathy.

Another important strategy for Indigenous grassroots candidates is their ability to speak to issues that are not just relevant to their communities but also to the broader public. Indigenous issues are often framed as separate from the rest of Canadian society, but the reality is that many of the challenges facing Indigenous people, such as poverty, unemployment, and environmental degradation, are also challenges that affect Canadians as a whole. Indigenous candidates can use this to their advantage by framing their policies in ways that address these broader issues while also advocating for the specific needs of Indigenous communities. This approach can help attract support from non-Indigenous voters who might otherwise not feel directly connected to Indigenous issues.

Indigenous candidates also often have a deep understanding of the importance of building coalitions and alliances. While they face unique challenges, they also have the potential to build powerful networks of support that transcend their communities. Many Indigenous communities have relationships with organizations and groups outside of their traditional territory that can provide valuable resources and support for their campaigns. By building these connections, Indigenous candidates can strengthen their campaigns and increase their chances of success. This ability to build alliances is particularly important in the context of a political system that has traditionally marginalized Indigenous voices.

The success of Indigenous candidates often depends on their ability to balance their responsibilities to their communities with the demands of running a campaign in a system that is not always receptive to their needs. This can be a delicate balancing act, as many Indigenous candidates are not just politicians but also community leaders, advocates, and caregivers. They have to stay connected to the people they represent while also navigating the political machinery necessary to win elections. This dual responsibility requires candidates to be deeply committed to their communities while also understanding how to operate within the broader political system. It's not an easy task, but it's one that many Indigenous candidates excel at, using their cultural knowledge, community ties, and passion for change to push for progress at all levels of government.

In the end, the challenges and successes of Indigenous candidates in Canada highlight the importance of representation, authenticity, and grassroots support. While they face significant barriers, they also bring valuable perspectives and strategies to the political table that can benefit not only their own communities but also all Canadians. By embracing their unique strengths and working to build coalitions with other like-minded groups, Indigenous candidates can inspire change and bring their voices into the political mainstream, helping to create a more inclusive and representative democracy.

Minority Representation

Minority representation in Canadian politics is often overlooked, but it's a crucial piece of the puzzle when it comes to grassroots candidates. Whether we're talking about racial minorities, LGBTQ+ individuals, or other marginalized communities, the road to political success is paved with unique challenges that aren't always visible to the public. These candidates often have to work harder to prove their worth, not just to the voters but to the party apparatus as well. Yet, despite these challenges, minority candidates often bring fresh perspectives and strategies that can shake up the political landscape.

For starters, minority candidates face the challenge of overcoming stereotypes and biases that are ingrained in society. This isn't just an issue at the voting booth but also within the political machinery itself. Parties and organizations, whether intentional or not, often overlook the value of minority voices, and that can make it harder for these candidates to gain traction. Whether it's the assumption that someone from a particular racial background won't be able to relate to a broader electorate or the reluctance to support a candidate who challenges traditional norms, minority candidates have to constantly prove they belong in the political conversation.

The challenge doesn't end there. For many minority candidates, simply getting their message out is a monumental task. Their voices are often drowned out by more mainstream candidates with larger budgets and more media exposure. Even if they have great ideas and a real connection with their community, they can still struggle to gain the attention of a broader electorate. Grassroots candidates from minority backgrounds may not have the same financial resources or institutional support as their more established counterparts, so they have to rely on their community ties and creativity to reach voters. This is where technology and social media come into play. A savvy minority candidate can use these platforms to amplify their voice, connect with potential voters, and build a sense of solidarity among like-minded individuals. Social media allows for direct engagement without the filters that traditional media often impose. It's an equalizer that gives marginalized voices the ability to reach out to voters without needing a massive budget to buy air time or print ads.

Another challenge faced by minority candidates is the need to address issues that are often seen as secondary by the mainstream political parties. While topics like the economy, healthcare, and national security tend to dominate the political discourse, minority candidates often feel a strong responsibility to address issues that are personal to their communities, such as systemic racism, access to education, and healthcare disparities. These are not issues that can be easily ignored, and minority candidates can bring a unique perspective to these discussions. By highlighting these issues, they not only raise awareness but also engage voters who feel that the mainstream parties are not listening to their concerns. This is a powerful way to build momentum, as it shows that the candidate is not just concerned with the general political agenda but is also deeply invested in the specific needs of their community.

Another unique strategy that minority candidates bring to the table is the ability to build coalitions with other marginalized groups. Political alliances in Canada are often formed along ideological or party lines, but minority candidates have the opportunity to form cross-community coalitions that can transcend traditional political boundaries. For example, a candidate from an immigrant background might find common ground with LGBTQ+ activists, environmentalists, or Indigenous groups who share similar concerns about social justice and inclusivity. These coalitions are valuable not just for pooling resources but also for creating a unified front that can challenge the status quo. It's a strategy that requires empathy, understanding, and the willingness to see beyond one's own community needs to create a broader vision of change.

The connection to the community is often the most powerful asset that minority candidates possess. They are deeply embedded in the struggles and aspirations of the people they represent, and that gives them a level of credibility that no amount of campaign ads or slogans can match. Minority candidates tend to be more visible and accessible within their communities, which allows them to build relationships and trust with voters. They often use this trust to mobilize supporters and volunteers, making their campaigns more resilient in the face of financial or logistical challenges. These grassroots networks are not only the backbone of their campaigns but also a source of their power. They provide a sense of belonging and solidarity, reminding people that their concerns matter and that their voices are worth hearing.

A significant part of the success of minority candidates lies in their ability to bring issues of diversity and inclusion to the forefront of political discourse. While mainstream parties may pay lip service to these issues, minority candidates often have the courage to tackle them head-on. Whether it's advocating for policies that address racial inequality, pushing for greater representation in the public sector, or challenging discriminatory practices, these candidates become symbols of resistance and change. Their success doesn't just help them individually; it opens doors for other marginalized groups to have a seat at the table as well.

Despite the challenges, the successes of minority grassroots candidates are significant. When they win, it's not just a victory for them personally but a victory for their community, too. It shows that change is possible, that the system can be challenged, and that a more inclusive and representative political system is within reach. The ability of minority candidates to navigate these complex dynamics and still succeed is a testament to their resilience, their commitment to their communities, and their determination to make a difference. They prove that representation matters and that diverse voices are essential for building a truly democratic society.

Ethnic and Cultural Diversity

Candidates from diverse ethnic and cultural backgrounds bring a unique set of strengths to the table, especially when it comes to building support within their communities. These candidates have an advantage because they are often intimately familiar with the experiences, concerns, and challenges that their communities face. They can connect on a deeper level because they share cultural ties, language, or similar lived experiences. This connection helps to build trust, and trust is a critical factor when it comes to getting people out to vote.

One of the most effective ways that candidates from diverse backgrounds can engage with their communities is through cultural understanding. When a candidate understands the traditions, values, and norms of the community they are seeking to represent, they are able to communicate in ways that resonate with voters. This can include everything from speaking in the same language to referencing cultural touchstones that have significance to the community. It also involves showing a genuine interest in the issues that matter to the community, whether it's access to healthcare, education, or dealing with social issues like discrimination and inequality. A candidate who understands these issues is more likely to gain the support of people who feel that mainstream politics does not address their needs.

Candidates can also engage with their communities by participating in cultural events and local activities. These events provide an opportunity for candidates to show up in person, interact with constituents, and demonstrate that they are not just a politician looking for votes but someone who is invested in the well-being of their community. Whether it's attending cultural festivals, religious gatherings, or local community meetings, these interactions help candidates to build a sense of belonging and increase their visibility. This kind of engagement is essential because it shows voters that the candidate is not just a figurehead but an active participant in the fabric of the community.

Furthermore, candidates can build support by highlighting the issues that are most relevant to their communities. For ethnic and cultural minorities, issues like discrimination, immigration policy, and cultural preservation are often top of mind. By openly addressing these concerns and showing that they understand the complexities of these issues, candidates can create a platform that resonates with their community. This means not only listening to people but also giving them a voice in the political conversation. It's not about simply pushing a political agenda, but rather about advocating for the needs of the people in a way that is rooted in their lived experiences.

One of the key ways that candidates from diverse backgrounds can foster support is through the power of storytelling. People connect with stories; they help to humanize candidates and make them relatable. A candidate who can share their personal journey or the struggles of their community is able to tap into the emotions of voters. Whether it's talking about the challenges of immigrating to Canada or the barriers they've overcome as a member of an ethnic minority, these stories serve as a bridge that connects the candidate to the people they aim to serve. It's not just about policy; it's about showing voters that the candidate truly understands their struggles and is committed to improving their lives.

Another crucial element for candidates from diverse backgrounds is building a network of support within their own community. This can mean working with local community organizations, faith groups, or grassroots organizations that already have the trust and attention of the community. By aligning themselves with these groups, candidates can build credibility and leverage the trust these organizations have worked hard to establish. These alliances also help candidates tap into existing volunteer networks, giving them the manpower they need to run an effective campaign. Additionally, these partnerships provide a platform for candidates to amplify their messages and increase their visibility among potential voters who may be otherwise disengaged from the political process.

Campaigning for support also involves listening, genuinely listening to the concerns of the community. Candidates who come from diverse ethnic and cultural backgrounds have an inherent advantage in this area, as they are often seen as more empathetic and more willing to represent their communities' interests. Listening to the community's concerns allows candidates to build their platforms in ways that are relevant and reflective of the needs of the people they want to represent. Moreover, this listening process can help identify gaps in services or areas where change is needed, allowing the candidate to offer solutions that are directly relevant to the issues that matter most.

By prioritizing cultural and community engagement, candidates can set themselves apart from others who may rely more heavily on traditional political strategies. This is especially important in areas with a high concentration of immigrants or ethnic minorities, where mainstream political parties may not have deep roots. A candidate from a minority background, however, is often in a better position to speak directly to the concerns of these communities and to offer solutions that feel authentic and relevant. This authenticity is essential in building long-term support, as voters are more likely to back a candidate who they believe genuinely understands and cares about their community's issues.

The combination of cultural sensitivity, community engagement, storytelling, and genuine listening creates a campaign strategy that resonates with voters. It's about showing up, speaking the truth, and engaging with the people in ways that are meaningful and impactful. Candidates from diverse backgrounds can use their unique position to not only build support within their own communities but also to help elevate those communities within the broader political conversation. Through these strategies, they not only create political change but also foster a more inclusive and representative political system that reflects the richness and diversity of Canadian society.

In recent years, there has been a noticeable shift in Canadian politics with younger and female candidates playing an increasingly vital role in grassroots campaigns. These candidates bring a fresh perspective and new energy to politics, challenging the traditional power structures that have long dominated the political landscape. For youth, especially, entering politics is not just about taking on established leaders; it's about reshaping the way we think about politics itself. The growing number of younger candidates has created space for bold ideas that are more reflective of the concerns of a younger generation, such as climate change, affordable housing, and student debt. These are issues that many older politicians have either failed to address or have only tackled in a piecemeal way. By running for office, younger candidates are forcing the conversation to evolve and creating a platform that speaks to the realities that younger Canadians face.

For women, especially in grassroots movements, the increasing participation in politics has been nothing short of revolutionary. Historically, politics has been dominated by men, and women have had to fight for a seat at the table. However, the rise of grassroots movements has allowed for greater inclusion of women who might have felt excluded from traditional political structures. Grassroots campaigns often operate on a smaller scale, with fewer barriers to entry, allowing women to make their mark without needing to navigate the same entrenched systems that often hinder their male counterparts. Grassroots campaigns are often more flexible and open to diverse voices, and this has led to an increase in the number of women running for office.

What's particularly powerful about younger and female candidates is the way they bring their lived experiences into the political conversation. Young people and women often have a very different perspective on life than the older, male-dominated political class. For young candidates, this often means advocating for policies that speak to the realities of modern life, such as affordable education, mental health resources, and employment opportunities. For women, this could mean advocating for policies that promote gender equality, improve childcare access, and address the specific challenges women face in the workplace or society at large. These candidates are not just running on traditional political platforms; they are running to bring about systemic change that reflects the diverse needs of Canadian society.

Additionally, both younger and female candidates often find themselves running for office with a more grassroots mindset. They understand that in order to be successful, they need to engage with people on a personal level, build relationships, and connect with voters in ways that traditional candidates may not. For younger candidates, this often means embracing new forms of communication, like social media, to speak directly to voters. Social media allows them to cut through the noise and present their messages in a way that feels personal and relatable. For women, running in grassroots campaigns often means working with local networks, engaging with organizations that support women's rights, and reaching out to communities that might otherwise be left out of the political conversation. They are often deeply connected to the issues that affect their communities and, as a result, are more likely to focus on policies that have real, tangible impacts on people's lives.

The role of younger and female candidates in grassroots campaigns also challenges the traditional power structures within political parties themselves. These candidates often bring with them a strong sense of independence and an unwillingness to simply toe the party line. In many cases, they challenge their parties to live up to the values they claim to represent. This can mean pushing for more progressive policies or questioning party leadership when it doesn't align with the needs of the people. Younger and female candidates often feel less beholden to the party establishment, giving them more freedom to advocate for what they believe in.

Moreover, the visibility of these candidates is helping to inspire a new generation of leaders. Seeing someone who looks like you or shares your experiences can be incredibly empowering. For young people and women, seeing candidates who represent them in politics can inspire them to get involved and take action. The more diverse the group of people running for office, the more inclusive the political process becomes, and this encourages participation from all sectors of society.

What's interesting about the rise of these candidates is not just that they are challenging the traditional power structures, but that they are also shifting the conversation about what it means to be a leader. For many people, leadership in politics has been associated with older, more established figures who have been in the system for years, if not decades. But younger and female candidates are showing that leadership isn't just about experience or seniority. It's about vision, energy, and a willingness to stand up for what's right, even when it's difficult.

They are showing that leadership can come from anywhere and anyone, and that fresh perspectives are not only valuable but necessary for the future of Canadian politics.

As the number of younger and female candidates continues to grow, their role in grassroots campaigns will become increasingly important. They will not only challenge the traditional power structures but also push for a political system that is more representative of the people it serves. These candidates are showing that politics can be a tool for change, a way to reshape the future and make it better for everyone, not just the elite few. Their involvement in grassroots movements isn't just about winning elections; it's about making sure that the voices of young people and women are heard and valued in the political process. This shift in political engagement, led by a diverse group of candidates, holds the promise of a more inclusive, dynamic, and forward-thinking political landscape for Canada.

Digital And Social Media

In today's political landscape, technology has become a powerful tool for levelling the playing field. For grassroots candidates, it offers an opportunity to reach a much wider audience without relying on the traditional, expensive methods of campaigning that have been dominated by the major political parties for so long. Digital and social media allow these candidates to bypass the media gatekeepers, directly engaging with voters in ways that were once unimaginable. With platforms like Facebook, Twitter, Instagram, and YouTube, a grassroots candidate can speak directly to the people, share their message, and build relationships without needing massive budgets. This opens up a whole new world of possibilities for candidates who might otherwise struggle to gain visibility in a crowded political landscape.

One of the most significant advantages of digital and social media is the ability to target specific groups of voters. With the help of tools like social media ads and targeted emails, grassroots candidates can tailor their messages to the issues that matter most to particular communities. This means they don't have to rely on generic, one-size-fits-all messaging. They can focus on the unique needs and concerns of different voter groups, whether it's a neighbourhood facing housing affordability issues or a community worried about the future of their local healthcare system. In the past, this would have required a massive advertising budget and media buy-ins, but now it's possible with relatively modest spending, especially when compared to the traditional political advertising costs.

Social media also allows candidates to build a more personal connection with voters. Instead of relying solely on speeches or interviews, candidates can share personal stories, interact directly with constituents through live streams, and provide behind-the-scenes glimpses into their campaign. This humanizes the candidate in a way that traditional media sometimes struggles to do. Voters get to see the candidate not just as a politician, but as a person who is genuinely engaged with the issues that matter to them. This can be incredibly powerful, especially in an environment where many people feel disconnected from traditional political systems and are craving more authenticity from their leaders.

What's also exciting about the rise of digital media is that it allows grassroots candidates to quickly respond to issues and capitalize on moments when they can connect with voters. For example, if a new development or controversy arises in the news, a candidate can post a response or opinion within hours. This immediacy creates a level of responsiveness that was not possible before. Voters are able to see that the candidate is engaged with current events and is actively participating in the ongoing conversation. This kind of responsiveness is crucial for building trust with the electorate and showing that a candidate is in touch with what is happening in the world around them.

Another benefit of digital media is that it empowers grassroots campaigns to mobilize supporters quickly and efficiently. Social media platforms that are good at connecting people are perfect for organizing events, raising funds, and getting people involved in the campaign. With just a few clicks, supporters can RSVP for an event, donate money, or share campaign materials with their networks. This creates a sense of community and involvement that can be crucial for getting people excited about a candidate. People who might not have the time or resources to physically attend a rally can still participate in the campaign by sharing posts, volunteering online, or spreading the word in their own networks.

The power of digital and social media is also in its ability to create viral moments that can quickly build momentum for a campaign. In the past, a campaign needed to rely on traditional media to spread a message. But now, a single tweet, video, or post can reach thousands, even millions, of people in an instant. Grassroots candidates, who may have limited resources, can now have the same viral potential as the major political parties. All it takes is one well-timed message that resonates with voters, and suddenly the campaign has gained national attention. This democratization of media has fundamentally changed the way campaigns are run, allowing even the smallest candidate to compete on a more equal footing with the larger parties.

Of course, digital media comes with its challenges. It can be difficult to cut through the noise and stand out among the flood of information people are exposed to every day. False information, trolls, and bots can easily spread disinformation that undermines a campaign's message. But for all its potential pitfalls, the role of technology in grassroots campaigns can't be overstated. It gives candidates the chance to compete in ways that were once unimaginable, levelling the playing field and allowing them to reach voters more effectively than ever before. It is an essential tool for grassroots candidates looking to make their mark in Canadian politics.

Electoral Reform

Electoral reform in Canada is a topic that has been debated for years, and for good reason. As it stands, Canada's first-past-the-post system tends to favour larger parties with well-established infrastructure and resources. Grassroots candidates, who often don't have the same level of funding or institutional backing, find themselves at a disadvantage in this system. Proportional representation and ranked-choice voting are two reforms that have the potential to level the playing field, making it easier for grassroots candidates to gain a foothold and ultimately succeed in elections.

Proportional representation is an electoral system that aims to match the percentage of votes a party receives to the number of seats it holds in the legislature. In this system, smaller parties and independent candidates have a much better chance of securing a seat, as their vote share is more directly reflected in the number of seats they win. For grassroots candidates, this is a huge advantage. Under the current system, if a candidate doesn't win the most votes in their riding, they don't win a seat, even if they have significant support. With proportional representation, the chances of smaller, grassroots parties gaining seats increases. This means that rather than being shut out of the political process, grassroots candidates can gain representation that aligns more closely with the actual support they've garnered.

Ranked-choice voting, on the other hand, allows voters to rank candidates in order of preference rather than choosing just one. This system helps prevent vote splitting, where multiple candidates with similar platforms divide the vote, often allowing a less popular candidate to win with a minority of the votes. For grassroots candidates, this can be particularly beneficial because it allows voters to express support for smaller parties or independent candidates without the fear that their vote will be "wasted." If a grassroots candidate is not the first choice for a voter, but is the second or third choice, that vote can still count toward them as preferences are redistributed. This encourages more diverse and nuanced campaigning, as candidates seek to build broad coalitions of support rather than simply targeting the most partisan voters.

Both proportional representation and ranked-choice voting could encourage more diverse voices in Canadian politics, especially at the grassroots level. These reforms would make it harder for larger parties to dominate, as smaller parties and candidates would have a better chance of breaking through. For grassroots campaigns, this is a game-changer. No longer would a candidate need to rely on a large, established party apparatus to win; they could build support in their local communities and still be fairly represented in the national conversation.

One of the biggest challenges that grassroots candidates face is breaking through the noise of the larger parties, which have more money, more resources, and more media attention. Proportional representation would allow these candidates to have a much more direct path to influence. A candidate who has significant local support but is running in a riding where they're unlikely to win under the first-past-the-post system could still be rewarded with a seat through proportional representation. This would allow candidates to build a national presence and even form coalitions with other like-minded candidates, further strengthening the impact of grassroots campaigns.

Ranked-choice voting, in particular, would encourage candidates to reach out to voters beyond their traditional base. Grassroots candidates often struggle to expand their voter base beyond a niche group of supporters. With ranked-choice voting, they can appeal to voters who might not agree with every aspect of their platform but are willing to support them as a second or third choice. This opens the door for a more inclusive form of campaigning, where candidates don't need to be entirely partisan or exclusive in their appeal.

Additionally, these reforms could encourage greater political engagement overall. When voters feel that their vote will actually count, they're more likely to turn out to vote. Right now, in many constituencies, people feel like their vote won't matter unless they vote for one of the major parties. Proportional representation and ranked-choice voting would change that dynamic, making elections more competitive and encouraging a wider range of voters to participate.

Grassroots candidates, who often have limited resources, could benefit immensely from these electoral reforms. With proportional representation, their support would be better reflected in the political system, making it easier for them to win seats and influence policy. Ranked-choice voting would allow them to appeal to a broader base and build coalitions, improving their chances of success even if they don't have the most popular platform in a given riding. Both systems have the potential to create a more inclusive, democratic system that truly represents the diversity of Canadian society. For grassroots candidates, this could be the key to a more level playing field in the future of Canadian politics.

Sustainability Of Grassroots Movements

Grassroots movements often face a difficult challenge: how to keep the energy alive once the election cycle ends. After a hard-fought campaign, it's easy for momentum to slow down or even dissipate entirely. If grassroots organizations want to succeed beyond just the election season, they need to think about long-term sustainability. This involves creating a structure that keeps people engaged, ensuring that their efforts have lasting impacts, and building a foundation that will support future candidates and campaigns.

One of the most important aspects of maintaining momentum is keeping the community engaged in meaningful ways. For many grassroots organizations, the election is just one part of a much larger struggle. If candidates and their teams stop connecting with their supporters after the campaign ends, it's hard to maintain any momentum. The key is to create ongoing engagement that goes beyond just voting. This can take the form of regular community events, local initiatives, or continued conversations on the issues that matter most to the people who supported the campaign. It's about showing that the work doesn't stop when the votes are counted. Grassroots organizations can maintain momentum by staying involved in their local communities, offering support on a variety of issues, and keeping their networks active and connected.

A major part of this sustainability is creating a solid, organized infrastructure that doesn't disappear once the campaign is over. Grassroots movements often rely heavily on volunteers, who may come and go depending on the level of excitement during an election. To ensure that momentum doesn't fade, it's crucial to build a structure that can keep people around, even when they aren't actively campaigning. This could mean organizing events that align with the values of the movement, creating committees for ongoing projects, or establishing local chapters that keep people involved year-round. The most successful grassroots organizations are those that maintain a sense of community and purpose, even when the spotlight of an election is no longer shining on them.

Fundraising also plays a critical role in sustaining a grassroots movement. Without the same access to corporate donations or big money as larger parties, grassroots organizations have to be creative in their funding efforts. This could mean relying on small donations from local supporters, crowdfunding, or organizing fundraising events that connect directly with the community. By building a donor base that feels personally invested in the movement, grassroots organizations can ensure that they have the resources they need to continue their work. This doesn't just help fund future campaigns but also supports long-term initiatives that align with the goals of the movement.

Building a lasting movement requires maintaining a focus on the issues that matter to people. If a grassroots organization is able to stay true to its mission and consistently advocate for the causes that inspired its creation, it will have a greater chance of staying relevant beyond the election cycle. This means not just reacting to current events, but staying proactive in addressing community needs and concerns. Grassroots organizations need to ensure that their work has tangible benefits for the people they serve, and that these benefits extend beyond the political cycle.

Another way to ensure sustainability is through developing leadership within the movement. Grassroots organizations rely on passionate individuals to drive the cause forward, but if leadership is limited to just a few people, the movement can falter when those leaders move on. By identifying and nurturing new leaders within the community, a movement can grow and thrive over time. Grassroots organizations should invest in training future leaders and empowering local communities to take ownership of the cause. This helps to build a deep, long-term connection with the community and ensures that the movement doesn't collapse when the original leadership steps back.

Finally, it's essential for grassroots organizations to stay adaptable. Political landscapes change, and so do the needs of the people. If a grassroots movement is rigid in its approach, it risks losing relevance as circumstances evolve. By being flexible and open to new ideas, grassroots organizations can stay responsive to the needs of the people they serve. This adaptability is critical in ensuring that the movement doesn't just survive but thrives in the face of changing political and social environments.

In the end, sustaining a grassroots movement isn't about a single campaign or a moment of victory. It's about building relationships, maintaining connections, and staying engaged with the community in a way that doesn't rely solely on election cycles. By creating infrastructure, staying focused on the issues that matter most, and empowering new leadership, grassroots organizations can remain a powerful force for change, even after the election is over.

Call To Action

If we want real change in Canada, the kind that genuinely addresses the issues affecting everyday people, we need to take action at the grassroots level. It's easy to feel disconnected from the political system, especially when we see the same faces and the same old ways of doing things. But if we're serious about making a difference, we can't just sit on the sidelines. We need to get involved, support grassroots efforts, and challenge the status quo. Grassroots campaigns are where the real potential for change lies because they are driven by ordinary people who care deeply about their communities. These are the campaigns that prioritize the issues that matter most to people, rather than the interests of big corporations or political elites.

Supporting grassroots efforts means more than just voting every few years. It means getting involved in local politics, attending town halls, volunteering for campaigns, and helping to organize events that raise awareness about the issues that need attention. Grassroots movements are powered by the energy and passion of everyday people who believe in the power of collective action. These movements aren't about big donors or corporate interests; they're about communities coming together to demand better, more responsive leadership. By supporting these efforts, we give voice to those who are often ignored by the mainstream political parties. We can help lift up candidates who are running on platforms that reflect our values, not those of the political establishment.

If we truly want to challenge the status quo, we need to think beyond the conventional political parties and their traditional ways of doing things. The existing political structures are often more focused on maintaining power than on solving the real problems people face. Grassroots candidates are different. They are not beholden to corporate interests or big-money donors, so they can focus on what truly matters: the needs and concerns of their constituents. By supporting these candidates, we not only challenge the current system but also help build a political landscape that is more inclusive, accountable, and responsive to the people it's meant to serve.

Engaging in politics is one of the most effective ways to make a real impact. Whether it's advocating for better public services, pushing for policies that address the affordability crisis, or supporting initiatives that promote environmental sustainability, local politics is where we can see the direct effects of our efforts. When we get involved, we have the chance to shape policies that will affect our daily lives, from the schools our children attend to the healthcare services available to us. Grassroots candidates are often the ones who understand these issues best because they live in the same communities, face the same challenges, and are directly accountable to the people they represent.

Now is the time for us to push for a political environment that is driven by people, not by money or corporate interests. Grassroots campaigns have the power to break down the barriers that prevent ordinary people from getting involved in politics. By supporting these campaigns, we take a stand against the forces that have entrenched power for so long. Grassroots candidates are already challenging the status quo, but they need our help. Our involvement can make the difference between a candidate running on a platform of real change and one who is more focused on maintaining the status quo.

If we want a government that truly reflects our values, we need to step up and demand it. The more we engage in local politics, support grassroots efforts, and push for candidates who represent our interests, the more we can change the political landscape in Canada. It's not enough to hope for change; we have to be the change. So, get involved, volunteer, support candidates who align with your values, and help spread the word. Together, we can build a political system that serves everyone, not just the powerful few.

Changing Political Landscapes

The future of grassroots candidates and campaigns in Canada will undoubtedly be shaped by a range of factors. One of the most significant will be the ongoing advancements in technology. We've already seen how social media, digital organizing, and data analytics have revolutionized how campaigns reach and engage with voters. In the future, technology will likely continue to play a central role, and it's hard to imagine grassroots campaigns succeeding without it. New platforms, tools, and technologies could enable candidates to connect with voters more directly and personally, regardless of geographical limitations. For instance, virtual town halls and live-streamed events may become the norm, allowing candidates to engage with voters in real time, even in the most remote corners of the country. These tools will make it easier for candidates to speak directly to the people they represent, listen to their concerns, and foster a sense of connection and involvement that's often missing in traditional, in-person politics.

At the same time, the demographic landscape in Canada is changing. Canada is becoming more diverse, and this shift will likely affect future campaigns in a variety of ways. As the population becomes increasingly multicultural, candidates will need to understand and address the specific needs and concerns of different communities. For grassroots candidates, this means broadening their outreach efforts and developing platforms that reflect the diverse interests of their constituents. It also means finding ways to create more inclusive campaigns that speak to the values of different groups while still maintaining a clear and unified vision. The rise of new communities in Canada also presents an opportunity for grassroots movements to tap into previously untapped voter bases, creating more opportunities for candidates to reach people who may not feel represented by the traditional parties.

Another trend that will likely impact future campaigns is the changing nature of voter engagement. We've seen in recent years that voter turnout can fluctuate depending on the level of enthusiasm and trust in the political system. As people become more frustrated with traditional politics, grassroots campaigns have an opportunity to provide an alternative. These campaigns can energize people who might otherwise feel disconnected from the political process by offering a more authentic, transparent, and accessible approach. Social media has already given candidates the ability to engage with voters on a more personal level, and in the future, this could expand even further. Candidates may use new digital tools to build relationships with voters in ways that feel more genuine and less transactional. The rise of direct, unfiltered communication between candidates and their supporters could make it easier to foster trust and enthusiasm.

That said, while technology can open up new possibilities, it also brings new challenges. The digital divide, where certain groups of people are left behind in terms of access to technology, will remain an issue. Grassroots campaigns need to ensure that they're not only relying on digital tools to reach voters. They must also continue to engage with people who may not have access to the internet or who prefer traditional methods of communication. The challenge for grassroots candidates will be balancing these different approaches and ensuring that they're meeting voters where they are, whether that's online, in person, or through more traditional channels like phone calls and direct mail.

The overall trend of polarization in politics could also shape the future of grassroots campaigns. As divisions grow wider between different political ideologies, grassroots candidates may find themselves in a position to either bridge these gaps or lean into them. On one hand, grassroots movements could work to create more unity by focusing on shared values and interests, building coalitions that span across traditional political lines. On the other hand, as political polarization intensifies, grassroots movements may find themselves in a position to harness that energy, tapping into the frustration of people who feel left behind by the status quo. Whether they lean into polarization or work toward unity, the future of grassroots campaigns will depend on how they navigate these tensions and connect with voters who are feeling increasingly disillusioned with traditional politics.

Finally, the changing role of money in politics will also play a significant part in shaping the future of grassroots campaigns. As fundraising continues to move online, it will become easier for grassroots candidates to raise money directly from their supporters, bypassing traditional fundraising channels that benefit the larger parties. Crowdfunding platforms and small-dollar donations could allow grassroots campaigns to run competitive races even without the deep pockets of more established parties. This could lead to more competitive, diverse candidates running for office and more opportunities for people who may not otherwise have the financial resources to mount a successful campaign.

In the end, the future of grassroots candidates in Canada will be determined by how they adapt to these changing political landscapes. Technology, demographics, voter engagement trends, and the role of money will all shape the way campaigns are run and how candidates connect with voters. The most successful grassroots candidates will be those who can harness these changes to create more inclusive, dynamic, and accessible campaigns that reflect the evolving needs and values of the Canadian electorate.

Final Thoughts

Grassroots politics plays a critical role in strengthening democracy by ensuring that the voices of everyday people are heard. When we look at the current political system, it's often easy to feel like the average citizen doesn't have much power. Big money, corporate interests, and entrenched political elites seem to hold the reins, and it can feel like we are just spectators watching from the sidelines. But grassroots politics changes that dynamic. It brings the power back to the people, allowing ordinary citizens to take action, build movements, and get involved in the political process in ways that truly reflect their needs and values. These movements aren't just about winning elections; they are about making sure that the decisions being made in government are genuinely representative of the diverse populations they are meant to serve.

In Canada, where the political landscape is becoming increasingly diverse, it's more important than ever to have candidates who represent the full spectrum of the population. Grassroots candidates are often the ones who can connect most authentically with the communities they represent. They aren't just speaking to issues from the top down. Instead, they come from the very communities they aim to serve, and they understand firsthand the struggles and challenges faced by people on the ground. This connection gives them a unique perspective and allows them to speak in a way that feels real and relevant to voters. When candidates come from grassroots movements, they bring a deep sense of accountability to the people they represent, which is something that can get lost in traditional top-down politics.

Grassroots campaigns also have a way of bringing new voices into the political process. They encourage diversity in representation, especially among groups that are often underrepresented in politics, whether that's women, racial minorities, Indigenous peoples, or younger generations. These candidates don't just run on traditional party platforms; they run on platforms shaped by the lived experiences of the communities they're a part of. This is important because it broadens the conversation and ensures that decisions aren't being made solely by those in positions of power or privilege. Grassroots candidates often challenge the status quo, pushing for policies that might not be on the agenda of mainstream political parties but that reflect the needs of those who are typically left out of the conversation. In this way, they help to build a more inclusive and representative democracy.

The beauty of grassroots politics lies in its ability to mobilize people who might otherwise feel disconnected from the political system. When people see candidates who are genuinely interested in representing their concerns, it can inspire a sense of hope and urgency that leads to greater political participation. Voters begin to realize that they do have power and that their voice matters. In a way, grassroots politics revitalizes democracy by showing people that their participation is vital and can lead to real change. It's through these movements that we can address the issues that matter most, from healthcare to education, environmental sustainability to economic equality.

At its core, grassroots politics is about more than just elections. It's about making sure that democracy is truly a system of the people, by the people, and for the people. When we focus on building movements that bring diverse voices into the fold, we're not just fighting for change in one election cycle. We're creating a foundation for a healthier, more representative, and more responsive democracy that will continue to evolve and grow. Grassroots candidates help to ensure that everyone's voice is heard, not just those with the most power or influence. That's what makes grassroots politics such an important part of the democratic process.